Mystery history of a
VIKING
LØNGBØAT

Fred Finney

Illustrated by Mike Bell and Roger Hutchins

COPPER BEECH BOOKS
BROOKFIELD, CONNECTICUT

© Aladdin Books Ltd 1997

Designed and produced by
Aladdin Books Ltd
28 Percy Street
London W1P 0LD

First published in
the United States in 1997 by
Copper Beech Books,
an imprint of
The Millbrook Press
2 Old New Milford Road
Brookfield, CT 06804

Editor
Jim Pipe
Designed by
David West Children's Books
Designer
Simon Morse
Illustrated by
Mike Bell – Specs Art
Roger Hutchins
Additional illustrations by
David Burroughs
Rob Shone
Gary Long

Printed in Belgium

Library of Congress Cataloging-in-
Publication Data
Finney, Fred, 1944-
Viking longboat / by Fred Finney ;
illustrated by Mike Bell ... [et al.]
p. cm. — (Mystery history of a—)
Includes index.
Summary: Describes life in the rough-
and-tumble world of the Vikings,
covering feasts, navigation, journeys,
rituals, and raids.
ISBN 0-7613-0590-4 (trade bdg.). —
ISBN 0-7613-0601-3 (lib. bdg.)
1. Vikings—Juvenile literature.
[1. Vikings.] I. Bell, Mike, ill. II. Series:
Mystery history.
DL 65.F55 1997   96-50173
909'.0439501—dc21   CIP AC

Contents

The Viking Longboat

This is a book about the Vikings. But it is also about the ship that made them so successful – the longboat (below). The "dragon ship," as it was called, lay at the heart of the Viking way of life. The Vikings depended on it for everything they did – whether raiding, trading, fishing, or searching for a place to live.

The ancient Egyptians could have built boats capable of crossing the Atlantic (above). But the 10-century Viking longboat was the first vessel to brave the stormy seas and complete the dangerous voyage to America. That's five hundred years before Christopher Columbus reached America in 1492.

This amazing boat was also light enough to be moved overland, or rowed up shallow rivers to unload a fearsome war party or a cargo of animals (below).

The Mystery of History

Much of what we know about the longboat comes from ships and other objects found in Viking graves, and from Viking sagas (stories). But there's still a lot we don't know. So as you read, try to imagine the sights, the sounds, and even the smells. Who knows, your picture of Viking life might be right. That's the real mystery of history!

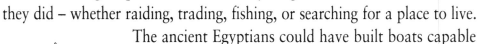

Using Mystery History

You'll find that *Mystery History of a Viking Longboat* is packed with puzzles and mysteries for you to solve. But before you go any further, read the instructions below to get the most out of the book!

Catch the Thief

*One of the Vikings has run off with the magic shield of Odin! No one knows who, but on page 29 some likely rogues are lined up. To help you work out which one of them is the thief, clues are given in the six Catch the Thief quiz boxes. For example, if you think **b** is the right answer, then it might tell that the thief is wearing a blue jacket. But you need to answer the questions correctly – and that means reading the book carefully. Happy hunting!*

Norse Puzzles

The sign of the Viking helmet marks a special puzzle that is anything from a maze to a message written in mysterious runes. Answers are given in Odin's Answers.

True or False

Some pages have a True or False question with an answer (on page 29) that may surprise you!

Loki's Quest

Try to find the objects hidden by the Norse trickster god Loki, then guess if they were around in the 10th-century Viking world!

History Mysteries

Around each page are questions like: **Q1 Did the Vikings only attack small places?** *Try to think about these, then look at Odin's Answers at the bottom of each page.*

Odin's Answers

Answers to Loki's Quest 🔍, *History Mysteries* **Q1**, *and Norse Puzzles* are given in this panel at the bottom of each page.

The Race Around the World Game

At the back of the book are full answers to Loki's Quest and True or False, a lineup of fierce-looking Vikings (one of whom has run off with Odin's magic shield), and, last but not least, a fantastic map of the Viking world that is also an exciting board game!

The Viking Raiders

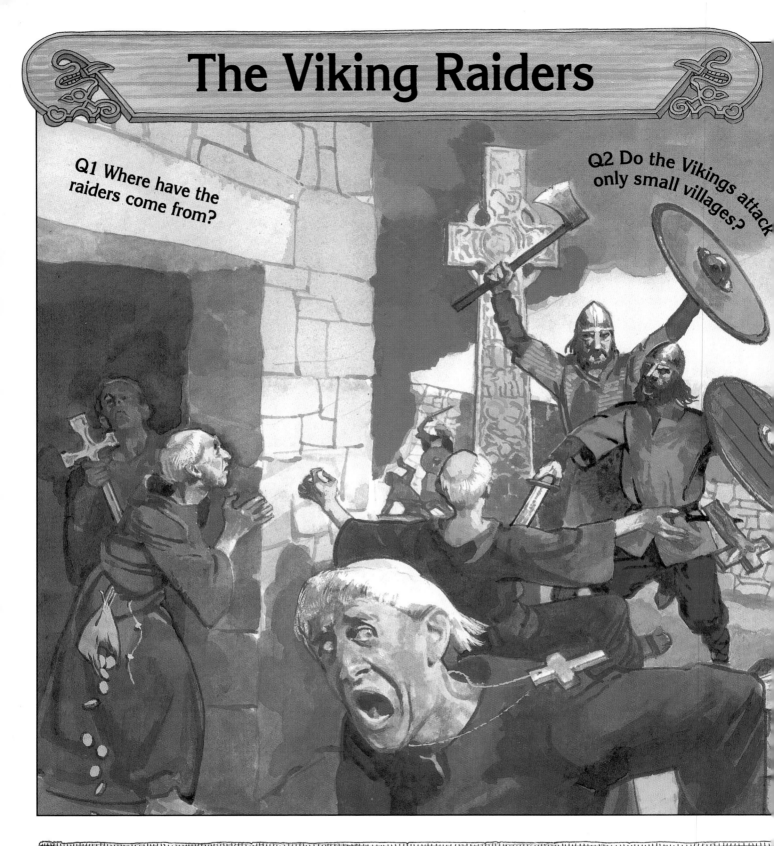

Q1 Where have the raiders come from?

Q2 Do the Vikings attack only small villages?

Odin's Answers

Q1 The Vikings (or Norsemen) come from Scandinavia, the lands that now make up the north European countries of Norway, Denmark, and Sweden. The Vikings attacking Lindisfarne are Norwegians, perhaps the most adventurous of the Viking peoples.

Q2 No. Viking armies attack big cities like London and Paris. Vikings also attack other ships at sea – the word *vikingr* means pirate.

But the Vikings aren't just raiders – many are farmers. Other Vikings build and develop trading towns such as Hedeby, Dublin, and Kiev.

Q3 Because they don't have time. The Vikings attack without warning, and before the defenders have time to gather an army, the Vikings have gone.

Though their victims describe them as brutal killers, in their own stories the Vikings are fair fighters: They will not attack someone already in a fight.

In A.D. 793, Viking ships suddenly appear at Lindisfarne monastery in the north of England. Taking the monks by surprise, they destroy the buildings by fire and steal their treasures. They seize the monks as slaves or throw them into the sea.

For the next three centuries, the Vikings terrorize northern Europe. Though they speak the same language, Old Norse, the Vikings are not one nation. During this period, groups of Vikings become the Swedes, the Danes, and the Norwegians. While the Swedes sail east to Russia and Byzantium in search of new goods, the Danes and the Norwegians sail west to England, Ireland, Iceland, and France, seizing lands wherever they can. But all Vikings rely on one vessel to achieve their purpose: the dragon-headed longboat!

🔲 *Loki's Quest*
Can you spot the catapult, horned helmet, female warrior, and coins? Which might you see in a Viking raid?

Q3 Why don't the monks run for it?

⚜ The Name Game

Vikings are often named after Norse gods and goddesses – such as Thor or Freya, while others are called animal names such as "ulf," meaning wolf, and "bjorn," meaning bear.

However, many famous Vikings were also given nicknames by later historians. Some of these names are not very polite: Eyvind Snake, Olaf the Stout, Bersi the Strong, Grjotgard the Nimble, Keith Flatnose, and Harald Finehair.

Can you guess who in the main picture might have been called Sigrid the Red?

⚜ Name Game Answer

Sigrid is the man with the red beard! Can you think of Viking-style nicknames for your friends? Perhaps you know a Naomi the Nimble, a Kate Curlylocks, a Tim the Terrible, or even a Gary Grumpyface?

turn to page 28.

🔲 *Loki's Quest Answer: You might see coins, and very occasionally, a female warrior. To find out why,*

The Dragon Ship

T he Viking longboat – the Dragon Ship – is a new and deadly weapon. No one before has built a boat to cut through the cold, rough seas of the north. They are built so they can be rowed forward and backward, and fierce dragons are carved on the prow to scare the gods of the Vikings' enemies. Vikings give their boats names like "Raven of the Wind" and "The Long Serpent."

Viking fighters do their own rowing, seated on chests, with oars that pass through holes in the boat's side. Their oars are the dragon's legs. The boat's square sail, often red and sometimes with a large black crow painted on it, is the dragon's wings.

Q1 Do the Vikings have compasses?

🜨 Which Ship?

Match **a**, **b**, and **c** with: a local fishing boat, a longboat (a *drakkar*) built for raiding, and a merchant ship built for cargo (a *knorr*). (*Hint:*Look at the scale.)

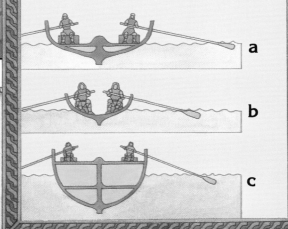

a

b

c

🜨 Which Ship Answers

The Vikings are master builders with a number of different boat designs suited to different tasks or waters. The 82-ft (25-m) longboat is built for speed, so it is narrow for a sea-going ship. The merchant knorr has extra decks to carry as much cargo as possible. The fishing boat is narrowest of all as it is only used in calmer waters close to land. So the answers are:
a *– Longboat,* ***b*** *– Small Fishing Boat,* ***c*** *– Merchant Ship.*

Q2 What can a bird teach a Viking sailor?

Q3 Do you get wet on a longboat?

Catch the Thief
Viking sailors find land by following:

a Seabirds = thief wears a hat, helmet, or scarf

b Radar = thief wears a cloak

c A compass = thief wears neither

Use your clue to work out who the thief is on page 29.

True or False?
The longest longboat is almost 330 feet long.

◘ Loki's Quest
Can you spot the anchor, padlock, map, plastic lunchbox, and rubber boots? Which might you see on a Viking longboat?

Odin's Answers

Q1 No. But they know roughly where they are from the movements of the sun, stars, winds, and flotsam (stuff that floats on water, often toward land). They also know the shapes of the coastline and leave information carved in stone where they land.

Q2 Birds can show where land is. They migrate in regular patterns and tend to head toward land and shallow water to find food. Floki discovered Iceland by releasing two ravens at sea and following their flight.

Q3 You get completely soaked! One Viking saga tells how for each seven men rowing, six bale water out to stop the boat from sinking. Many Vikings die of cold and damp, and their bodies are thrown over the side.

◘ *Loki's Quest Answer:* You'd only see the anchor and padlock. To find out why, turn to page 28.

The Norse Gods

The Viking warriors have returned from a raid, and are giving thanks to their gods for the treasure they have captured. The Vikings have no special religious buildings, and worship wooden images of their gods out in the open. Before praying, they make offerings of bread, onions, milk, meat, and beer.

The Vikings are very religious and pray for help in all matters. Their gods are models for their warriors – brave, cruel, and easily angered. So if a Viking behaves cruelly, he is merely following the example set by the gods themselves.

Q1 Who is the most popular god?

Q2 Do the Vikings sacrifice animals?

◘ *Loki's Quest*
Can you see the scales, hot water bottle, golden Buddha statue, and abacus? Which might you see in a Viking settlement?

◘ *Loki's Quest Answer*
You might see the golden Buddha and the scales. To find out why, turn to page 28.

Odin's Answers

Q1 Thor is the most popular god. He makes thunderbolts with his mighty hammer, called Mjöllnir, which always flies back to his hand after he has thrown it. He also has an iron belt that makes the wearer twice as strong, and a pair of iron gloves.

Q2 Yes. The gods Odin and Frey demand sacrifice. At one feast, held every nine years, nine heads are offered of every type of living animal – including humans. Victims are killed with a sword and hung from a sacred tree. After prayers, the feasts begin. King Hakon even sacrificed his son.

⚔ Going to Valhalla

A Viking warrior believes that if he dies bravely in battle, he will go to Valhalla (Viking heaven), a hall with 640 doors! Can you find the quickest way to Valhalla through the maze below? On your way, you will meet the most important Norse gods. Every time you meet a god, you must change the color of your path. (*Hint:* For the quickest route, avoid Loki, the god of lies.)

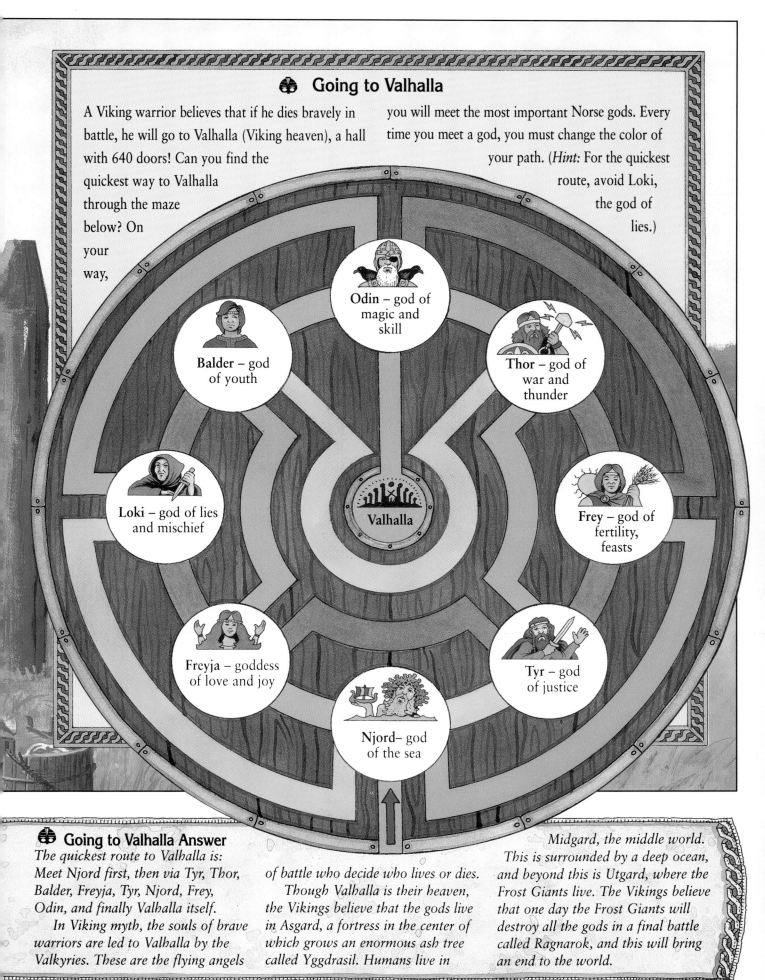

Odin – god of magic and skill

Balder – god of youth

Thor – god of war and thunder

Loki – god of lies and mischief

Valhalla

Frey – god of fertility, feasts

Freyja – goddess of love and joy

Tyr – god of justice

Njord– god of the sea

⚔ Going to Valhalla Answer

The quickest route to Valhalla is: Meet Njord first, then via Tyr, Thor, Balder, Freyja, Tyr, Njord, Frey, Odin, and finally Valhalla itself.

In Viking myth, the souls of brave warriors are led to Valhalla by the Valkyries. These are the flying angels

of battle who decide who lives or dies.

Though Valhalla is their heaven, the Vikings believe that the gods live in Asgard, a fortress in the center of which grows an enormous ash tree called Yggdrasil. Humans live in

Midgard, the middle world. This is surrounded by a deep ocean, and beyond this is Utgard, where the Frost Giants live. The Vikings believe that one day the Frost Giants will destroy all the gods in a final battle called Ragnarok, and this will bring an end to the world.

Viking Traders

Though they certainly enjoy raiding and piracy, most Vikings are not professional soldiers. They are farmers for much of the year, growing crops, and raising animals. Others, especially the Swedes, are great traders. Here you can see the bustling Danish port of Hedeby, protected by a long wooden wall. Merchants have come from all over Europe to sell their wares. The Vikings buy luxury goods from the East, like silk and spices, and in return sell natural products found in Scandinavia, like iron ore and furs.

The secret of the Vikings' trading success is thin ships. Here, it is spring, and ships are being built and repaired. The trunk of a tall tree is used as a keel, and end-pieces and overlapping planks are nailed to it.

Q2 Does anyone want the Vikings living near them?

Q1 What are Arab traders doing in Hedeby?

▣ Loki's Quest
Can you spot the drains, inflatable raft, shopping cart, traffic lights, and garbage cans? Which of these might you see in a Viking town?

Odin's Answers

Q1 Buying and selling, like everyone else! The Arabs (can you see any?) are great traders and bring with them goods from faraway places like India and China. One Arab merchant, Ibrahim Al-Tartushi, visits Hedeby in A.D. 950 and writes that it is known from Iceland to Baghdad.

However, he isn't very impressed with Hedeby – he complains that the buildings are poor and there is little treasure in the town.

Q2 Believe it or not, sometimes they welcome them! The Swedes are as well known as traders and builders as farmers and warriors. They bring their great practical skills to many areas and often end up blending in with the local people like the Slavs and the Bulgars.

▣ *Loki's Quest Answer: None of them! To find out why, turn to page 28.*

Catch the Thief
What do the Vikings call their longboat?

a Knorr = thief has fair hair
b Drakkar = thief has brown hair
c Dragonnar = thief has gray hair

Use your clue to work out who the thief is on page 29.

True or False? The Vikings give their weapons names.

🜲 Trading Puzzle
Can you spot people selling pots, amber beads (*below right*), combs (*below right*), cloth, beer, weapons, and slaves; and the town's cobbler, stonemason, butcher, fishmonger, window-maker, and blacksmith? But two traders won't sell much in Hedeby. Which two? (*Hint:* They're selling things found in buildings.)

🜲 Trading Puzzle
All these traders would do well at Hedeby, except the stonemason and the window-maker. Most Vikings buildings made of stone were simple affairs, not like the grand temples of Rome or the magnificent churches of Byzantium. So, there was little need for a mason to make fancy stone columns. No Viking houses had windows, let alone the fine stained-glass windows found in churches throughout medieval Europe.

Sailing to Byzantium

Q3 Are longboats attacked on the way to Byzantium?

Q1 The Rus have no farmland, so how do they live?

Odin's Answers

Q1 By trading in slaves and furs. During the winter, they trap animals for fur and kidnap men and women to sell as slaves. In the summer, they sail toward Byzantium, selling their booty on the way. Slave traders are said to be the richest of all merchants.

Q2 The Vikings know how to ride, but in many parts of Scandinavia it is quicker to travel by boat. However, in battle, they prefer to use Magyars (the founders of modern Hungary) in their cavalry. The skillful Magyars can ride in formation and shoot an arrow while at full gallop.

Q3 Yes, Viking boats are attacked on their way to Byzantium. But when the Swedish Viking Rurik becomes governor of the town of Novgorod in the late 9th century, he sets up armed camps and trading posts along the main routes. Later, Oleg the Wise builds warships to patrol the rivers.

Q2 Why don't the Vikings travel on horseback?

True or False?
The Vikings sell child slaves for huge sums of money.

The Swedes are so well-organized that in A.D. 862 the Slavs ask them to come and rule their country! These Vikings become known as the "Rus," and soon control a large part of what is now Russia. Their flat-bottomed longboats are perfect for sailing on the Russian lakes and rivers that lead south to Byzantium, the great Christian empire.

In A.D. 907, the Byzantines panic when Oleg the Wise leads a huge force of Viking ships and soldiers to the gates of Constantinople (called *Miklagard*, or "great city," by the Vikings). Here the Byzantine Emperor is giving Oleg a huge sum of money and the right to trade throughout his empire. Now the Viking traders are even closer to the spices and silks of the East.

⚜ White Water!

The Viking route from Sweden to Byzantium is full of danger. After crossing the stormy Baltic Sea, the longboats sail or row across lakes and down rivers to the Black Sea. However, not all waterways connect up to each other, and some rivers have terrifying rapids that can smash a boat to pieces.

BALTIC SEA · Kiev · Volga River · Dnieper River · BLACK SEA · CASPIAN SEA · Byzantium

How do you think the Vikings get around this problem? (*Hint:* The picture on the left should give you a clue.)

⚜ White Water!

If they come across a large rock in the river, the Vikings strip off their clothes, jump in the water, and move the boat near the bank. Then they guide the ship past with poles. To clear rapids and waterfalls, the boat is pulled out of the water. Using logs as rollers, it is dragged across land until it can be eased back into the water at a safe spot.

◯ Loki's Quest Answer: *You'd only see the ivory in Byzantium. To find out why, turn to page 28.*

Down on the Farm

The tough Vikings brave the stormiest seas and the fiercest opponents – but they still like to live in a homey way. These typical Viking homes are made on a frame of wooden posts, with walls made of mud and straw. The roof is covered with wood shingles, straw, and grass turf. Sometimes the houses are grouped together in a village or fort.

The Vikings keep cows, pigs, sheep, and goats – sometimes even in their own houses. The houses have no windows and smoke rises straight up from the central fireplace through a hole in the roof. Here they cook meat and fish (which they smoke, dry, or salt to eat during the long hard winter) and turn their barley and oats into bread, beer, and porridge.

Catch the Thief

What are Viking houses made of?

a Bricks = Thief has red boots

b Wood/straw = Thief has brown shoes

c Stone = Thief has blue/green shoes

Use your clue to work out who the thief is on page 29.

Q1 Why don't Vikings wear togas, like the Greeks and Romans?

Q2 Why are Viking winters so long?

Odin's Answers

Q1 Wraparound clothes like togas and saris have always been worn in hot countries, but they won't keep your legs warm in the cold. Viking men wear pants made from wool or leather, sometimes with foot pieces attached at the bottom (like tights today). To keep extra warm, they wind strips of cloth around their legs. They also wear jerkins (a type of thick jacket) and cloaks. Viking women wear woolen dresses, sometimes with two slits close to the breasts for nursing their babies. Shoes and boots are made from leather.

Q2 The closer you get to the North Pole, the longer the winters are, because the North Pole of the Earth tilts away from the Sun for this half of the year. Some Norwegians live far in the north, and have long winters – and long nights. Sometimes there are only one or two hours of daylight!

Feeling Hungry

The Viking diet is largely based on meat because the cold climate often means poor harvests. When food is scarce, which of the following would a hungry Viking eat?

bread

oranges

herring

seagull

horse

fox

seaweed

Loki's Quest
Can you spot the sauna, pogo stick, saw, plow, and reindeer herd? Which might you see on a Viking farm?

Q3 Why should these puffins look worried?

Q3 Because like most birds, puffins are a favorite Viking food. They often live on ledges below the cliff tops. Hunters lower themselves on ropes over the edge of the cliff and catch the birds with their hands or with nets. They also collect eggs and feathers and down for bedding.

Feeling Hungry Answers

Fish (like herring) and bread are basic foods. So are seagulls, easily caught and tasty in stews, and seaweed. But in the long winters, when supplies are scarce, the Vikings eat bread made from flour, peas, pinetree bark – and grit! They also eat anything they can catch: foxes, ravens, and even the family horse. The only thing they wouldn't eat are oranges, which only grow in hot countries.

Loki's Quest Answer: You'd see everything except the pogo stick. To find out why, turn to page 28.

Rough Justice

Q1 Why are these two men fighting?

Q2 What is it like to be a Viking woman?

Loki's Quest
Spot the skis, mug, toboggan, and ice skates? Which might you see in the Viking world?

True or False?
Some men earn a living from duels.

Odin's Answers

Q1 People fight duels (called *holmganga*) in order to settle a quarrel. The Vikings believe that duels – like everything else – are controlled by the gods, and the gods will see that justice is done. They are often fought on deserted islands, well away from the main settlement.

The *holmganga* has strict rules, and a referee watches the fight. It is fought on a cloak 10 ft (3 m) square.

If either man steps off the cloak, he is a coward. Each man may use up to three shields, and if he is wounded, he may withdraw. However, if one of the pair dies, the other gets all his property, so duels are often fought to the death. Sometimes a woman will promise to marry the winner of a duel.

Loki's Quest Answer:
You'd see all but the mug. To find out why, turn to page 28.

out why, turn to page 28.

Viking society is divided into *jarls* (chiefs and military leaders), *karls* (the freemen who own their own land), and *thralls* (slaves). Kings are elected by other chiefs at big assemblies, called *Things*, where laws were also carried out. There are no prisons and criminals pay a fine instead. But the laws don't stop the Vikings fighting among themselves. If anyone is killed in a fight, their family kills in revenge. Such senseless killing can go on for years.

Catch the Thief

What is a thrall?

a A type of Viking cloak = Thief has red/blue jacket

b A Viking battleax = No jacket

c A Viking slave = Green jacket

Use your clue to work out who the thief is on page 29.

✦ *Havamal* Puzzle

The *Havamal* is a set of poems that tells Vikings how to behave. Can you guess which two pieces of advice below are *not* part of the *Havamal*?

• Always treat your slaves nicely.

• Beer makes you stupid.

• Do not laugh at the old and gray, they may have something wise to say.

• Look around a doorway before you step in (*left*).

• When a guest arrives give them a bath and a nice warm seat.

• Never start a fight.

Q2 Viking women are not as free as men, though they often have great responsibility for running the farm while the husband is away trading or fighting. Viking women are protected by law. A girl of 15 may choose her own husband, and if he treats her badly, she can divorce him.

✦ *Havamal* **Answers**

The two sentences that are not part of the Havamal are the first and last. The Viking freemen (called karls) often behave very cruelly toward the slaves (thralls). They believe that some people are just born to be slaves. Slaves have no rights and no property, but if they work very hard, they can buy their freedom. And, of course, Vikings never have any worries about starting a fight!

Q1 Do the Vikings like reading?

Q2 What else do the Vikings do during the long, cold winters?

The Vikings are a violent and, at times, bloodthirsty people. But they are also great artisans. They know how to build wonderful boats and strong buildings out of wood. In this house, artists are working together, making fine weapons and beautiful jewelry out of metal, and carving wonderful shapes in wood and ivory. When the weather is bad, it is a good way of passing the time.

Viking patterns are bold and often show animal shapes stretched into fantastic shapes. The "gripping beast" design has dozens of animals all holding onto each other. These patterns are sometimes used to decorate Viking longboats, especially those used to bury important people.

○ Loki's Quest
Spot the radiator, iron, buttons, and the man putting on makeup. Which wouldn't you see in a Viking house?

Odin's Answers

Q1 Not really. Though runes (Viking letters) are used to carve messages on wood and stone, Vikings don't write on paper and don't have any books. Their great stories, called sagas, are spoken and are only written out later by descendants like Snorri Sturluson, a 13th-century poet. Like 20th-century rap, Viking poetry has a strong rhythm, using repeated consonants to create a strong beat.

Q2 They play games. Favorites are a ball game called *knattleikr*, board games, wrestling, and juggling with knives. However, even when playing, the Vikings are violent. In swimming competitions, contestants try to drown each other, and ball games can lead to arguments and fights.

○ *Loki's Quest Answer: You wouldn't see the radiator or buttons. To find out why, turn to page 28.*

True or False?

Runes can protect a Viking against witches.

Catch the Thief

Which Vikings are more famous for trading than raiding:

a Swedes = Thief has beard

b Danes = Thief has mustache

c Norwegians = Thief has no beard or mustache

Use your clue to work out who the thief is on page 29.

🌀 Runes

The Vikings write messages with mysterious letters called runes. Look at the rune alphabet (called a *futhark*) below and work out the names carved around the edge of this stone.

a	b	d	e	f	g	h	i	k,c	l	m

n	o	p	r	s	t	u,v,w	x	y	z

🌀 Rune Puzzle

The names around the stone are Sigrid, Floki, Freda, and Astrid. Now try to write your own name or message with runes. The Vikings leave rune graffiti wherever they go. (Who wrote the graffiti on page 12?) Rune stones are put either side of a river to show where to cross (as on page 14). The Vikings believe that someone who knows the runes can use them to protect themselves in battle.

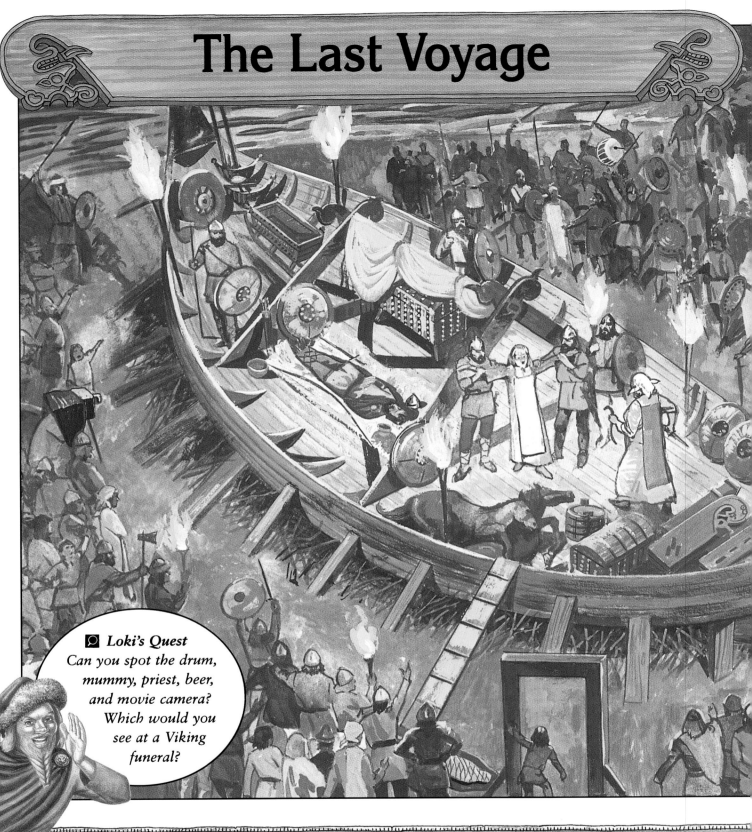

The Last Voyage

Loki's Quest
Can you spot the drum, mummy, priest, beer, and movie camera? Which would you see at a Viking funeral?

Odin's Answers

Q1 Not many. When the Catholic Church forbids Christians to trade with non-Christians, some Vikings start to wear crosses (but they still worship the Norse gods). Around A.D. 1000, King Olaf Tryggvason introduces Christianity to Norway, Greenland, and Iceland. The Icelanders vote to become Christian, but in Norway, some Vikings only become Christians after they are tortured.

Q2 In Russia, a slave girl will agree to be buried with her master because she will travel with him to Valhalla. She drinks and celebrates, and goes on board the funeral ship. While drunk, she is strangled. Then an old woman known as the "angel of death" thrusts a dagger into her heart.

Loki's Quest Answer: You'd see only the beer and perhaps the drum. *To find out why, turn to page 29.*

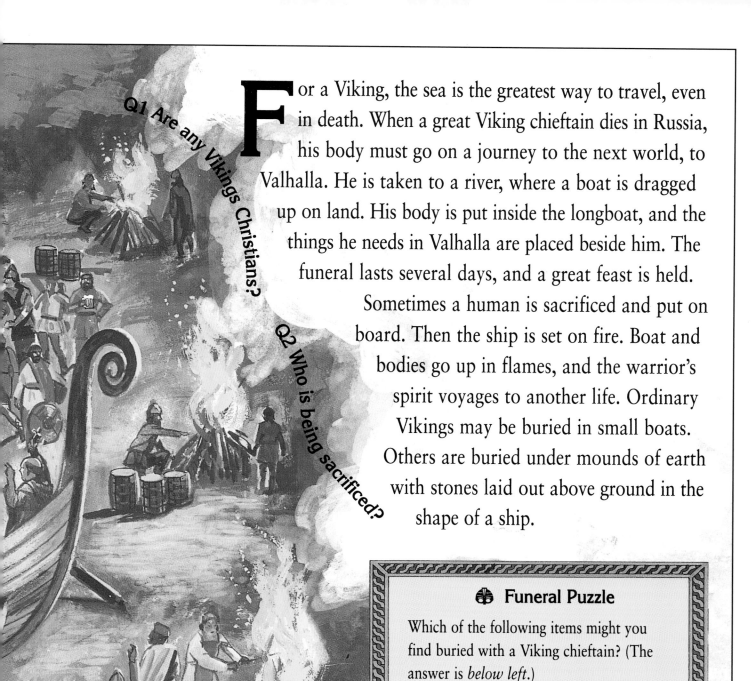

Q1 Are any Vikings Christians?

Q2 Who is being sacrificed?

For a Viking, the sea is the greatest way to travel, even in death. When a great Viking chieftain dies in Russia, his body must go on a journey to the next world, to Valhalla. He is taken to a river, where a boat is dragged up on land. His body is put inside the longboat, and the things he needs in Valhalla are placed beside him. The funeral lasts several days, and a great feast is held. Sometimes a human is sacrificed and put on board. Then the ship is set on fire. Boat and bodies go up in flames, and the warrior's spirit voyages to another life. Ordinary Vikings may be buried in small boats. Others are buried under mounds of earth with stones laid out above ground in the shape of a ship.

✠ Funeral Puzzle

Which of the following items might you find buried with a Viking chieftain? (The answer is *below left*.)

Bucket

Sled

Ax

Dog

Bed

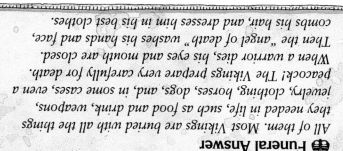

✠ Funeral Answer

All of them. Most Vikings are buried with all the things they needed in life, such as food and drink, weapons, jewelry, clothing, horses, dogs, and, in some cases, even a peacock! The Vikings prepare very carefully for death. When a warrior dies, his eyes and mouth are closed. Then the "angel of death" washes his hands and face, combs his hair, and dresses him in his best clothes.

The Great Fleets

The Danish and Norwegian Vikings are looking west. Instead of small raids, they begin to attack with armies of soldiers led by great warlords. The Vikings sail stealthily along the coasts and up the rivers. They attack and sometimes destroy large towns such as Cambridge in England, and even lay siege to Paris. By the end of the 9th century, they have conquered half of Anglo-Saxon England and large parts of northern France.

The Norwegians attack Cadiz in Muslim Spain, but are defeated by the Saracen fleet near Gibraltar in the Mediterranean. Here the Viking boats, weighed down with plunder, are being surrounded by the smaller but faster Saracen boats. Sea battles are fought like land battles, with the ships often roped together to form long lines.

Q1 Who fights in the huge Danish armies?

✵ Berserk Puzzle

The most feared Vikings are the *berserkirs*. Dressed in bearskins (*below*), they fight with great ferocity, and show no fear. Can you see any in the main scene? Before battle they even chew their shields. Maybe they chew agaric, a toadstool that sends them into a rage.

Some *berserkirs* forget they are not on land and rush at the enemy, fall overboard, and drown! What do you think the term "to go berserk" means today?

✵ Berserk Answer

Berserk is a Viking word which meant "bearcoat," but now means "battle-crazy." That's why today we talk about people who get mad or angry as "going berserk." *According to Viking stories, you couldn't learn to be a berserkir – you inherited the condition from your father!*

Odin's Answers

Q1 The warriors of the great raiding armies come mostly from towns. They fight for a share of the treasures they capture. Viking farmers, who might go on smaller raids, rarely want to spend years away from home as part of a big army.

Catch the Thief
Who or what is Valhalla?

a A Viking leader = Thief is wearing pants

b Viking heaven = Thief is wearing leggings

c Viking assembly = Thief is wearing a dress

Q2 How do the Danes attack big cities like Paris?

Loki's Quest
Can you spot the flag, chainsaw, flamethrower, and spurs? Which might you see in a Viking sea battle?

Q3 Who are the Saracens?

Q2 Using a combination of cunning and force. Longboats have a shallow draft (the depth of the boat lying under the water level) so they can be rowed far inland. In A.D. 885, 700 Viking ships and 30,000 Danes surround Paris, which is on an island. On the first night they set fire to the city and for weeks attack fiercely, including a huge assault on Easter Day, when they hope their Christian enemies will be busy at prayer. Then the Vikings try to starve them out – for a whole year. In the end, the city is saved and the Danes move south to plunder other lands.

Q3 "Saracen" is a medieval word for the Muslim Arabs who conquered most of the Middle East, North Africa, and Spain in the 7th–8th centuries A.D.

Loki's Quest Answer: The only thing you might see is a flamethrower! Find out why on page 29.

West Across the Atlantic

The Norwegian Vikings are always looking for good farming land. In A.D. 815, Floki of Rogaland sails his longboat on a long, hard voyage into the mid-Atlantic where he sets two ravens free. These birds lead him to the island of Iceland (see map, page 30). The 10,000 settlers that follow Floki group themselves into small communities run by Things.

In the next 100 years, the population of Iceland reaches about 30,000 people. There are now so many settlers that every year at midsummer, the heads of each family meet at the Althing, which is a great parliament and festival. Here they are in the middle of a fierce debate.

Q1 Do Things stop Vikings from fighting each other?

Q2 Do all the settlers stay in Iceland?

Odin's Answers

Q1 No. Things have no power to make anyone follow their decisions. Though there is a very strong feeling of community among the Icelandic Vikings, even the Althing can do nothing to stop violent quarrels, which often turn into family warfare.

Q2 No. In 982, a troublesome Viking called Eric the Red, who was wanted for some killings, sails even further northwest to Greenland (see map, page 30). Soon, 25 ships follow and two colonies are founded. The weather is so harsh that settlers sink their houses into the earth so far that only the green turf roofs are showing above the ground.

Settlers have to ship metal, timber, and grain from Norway, but they send back wool, fur skins, hides, and walrus ivory. As trees can't grow in Greenland, there is no wood for making fires. The settlers dry moss and heather and burn them instead.

⚜ Hunting Puzzle

Moose

Narwhal

Walrus

The Greenland Vikings are the first people to hunt whales, which often overturn their ships. It takes up to 15 men to kill a whale (*below*). The Greenlanders can only live by selling furs and walrus ivory to Norway. They even pretend to have magical unicorn horns for sale! Which animal in this panel does the horn really come from?

🔲 Loki's Quest
Can you spot the lawn mower, golf player, witch, bell ringers, and polar bear? Which might you see in Viking Iceland?

Q3 Actually, Iceland is quite green but Greenland is mostly ice! Eric the Red, who discovers Greenland, probably decides to give the country a nice name to encourage other settlers to follow him. Such lies may also explain why later Vikings call Newfoundland (a large island off North America) "Vinland" (Wineland) when they find it, even though the climate is far too cold to grow grapevines.

🔲 *Loki's Quest Answer: The only thing you might see is the witch! To find out why, turn to page 29.*

⚜ Hunting Answer
The narwhal. Its spiral tusk is a single tooth, 8 feet (2.5 m) long. Medieval people believe that anyone who drinks from a unicorn horn is protected from poisoning. Queen Elizabeth I of England (1533–1603) kept a unicorn horn (narwhal tooth) under her bed!

The Vikings in America

Q1 What is the journey like across the Atlantic?

Q2 How do we know the Vikings reached America?

Q3 What happens to the Vikings?

True or False?
The skraelings have no milk.

Odin's Answers

Q1 Horrible. It takes great courage to cross the ocean in a boat 80 ft (25 m) long when the waves can reach 100 ft (30 m) high. It is cold and cramped on board, though passengers have a leather sleeping bag. They live off salted fish and beer or sour milk.

Q2 It's all described in a Viking saga, and a Viking site has been found in the north of Newfoundland, Canada. It is called L'Anse-aux-Meadows (see map, page 30).

Here there are the remains of eight buildings and thousands of objects. Many of these were made of wood and were luckily preserved in a peat bog.

Radio carbon dating has shown these to be the right period for the Vikings and many of the objects are made in the Viking style. It seems that the 60 or so Vikings who lived here didn't stay for long.

Loki's Quest
Can you spot the leopard skin, horse, turkey, and paper money? Which don't belong in 10th-century America?

R estless and fearless, the Norwegians sail farther west. In about A.D. 992, Leif Ericson ("the Lucky") and Thorvald, both sons of Eric the Red, sail down the coast and see Helluland (Baffin Island), Markland (Labrador), and finally the green hills of Vinland (Newfoundland).

They come back with another expedition. The island is inhabited by an Algonquin tribe (called *skraelings* by the Vikings). In some fighting, Thorvald is killed and the Vikings leave. Another Viking, Thorfinn, sets out with 170 others. Here they are trading with the Algonquin, but soon fighting breaks out again. The Vikings never return to North America, and by A.D. 1100, the Viking age is over. Many of the Viking raiders settle down, while others find new land to farm in Scandinavia. But the tales of Viking heroes and their "Dragon ships" live on.

🜨 An American Mystery

How far inland did the Vikings go? Some historians believe they may have reached the Missouri River (that's 900 miles from the ocean).

Perhaps no one will ever solve this history mystery. However, one thing is certain about the Vikings – thanks to their remarkable longboats, they were one of the most adventurous people of all time.

A Viking carving of a Native American warrior (right).

Q3 Many Vikings become Christians in the 11th century, and settle down to a more peaceful way of life. Meanwhile, raiding gets harder as their enemies get more organized.

Wherever the Norsemen settle, they adopt the language and customs of the local people. Today, their descendants live in Norway, Sweden, Denmark, England, France, and Russia.

In parts of Europe, some Viking customs still remain: In the Shetland Isles (north of Scotland), people still perform a Viking ceremony called *Up Helly Aa* every January, by pushing a burning longboat out to sea. In some languages, even the days of the week are named after Norse gods. In English, for example, Wednesday is named after the god Woden.

Loki's Quest Answer: The only thing you might see is the turkey. To find out why, turn to page 29.

A Hoard of Answers

Loki's Quest

Pages 4–5

Large *catapults* had been used by the ancient Greeks, and were known to the Vikings, but they wouldn't have been taken on small raids. Vikings are often shown in pictures wearing *horned helmets* (*left*), but they never wore them (except possibly in one religious ceremony). *Female warriors* were rare among Vikings, though a famous female *berserkir* fought off a Native American war party. Vikings occasionally used pieces of silver and Arab and Roman *coins*, but they preferred to barter (exchange goods).

Pages 6–7

The Vikings had *anchors*, complete with metal chain links. *Padlocks* like this one (*right*) were often used by Vikings to lock up their possessions. The Vikings had some very simple *maps,* but they wouldn't have helped much in navigation. Plastic wasn't invented until the 19th century, so the *plastic lunchbox* is right out of place. Vikings probably kept their food in pots or wrapped in cloth while traveling. Rubber wasn't used for boots until the 19th century. The first *rubber boots* were made in the same style as the leather boots worn by the English general, the Duke of Wellington.

Pages 8–9

Scales (*right*) have been found in Viking graves. They were especially important for traders dealing in precious metals. *Hot water bottles* made of rubber did not appear until the 19th century. To keep warm as a Viking, you wrapped up snugly and slept near a fire! A bronze figure of a *golden Buddha* was found in one of the Viking trading posts. The *abacus* was invented in the Near East thousands of years ago, but there is no evidence that the Vikings used them.

Pages 10–11

Drains were known in the Indus valley (today's Pakistan) in 2500 B.C. – but the Vikings just shoveled their sewage into a pit. The first *inflatable raft*, made from canvas and rubber, was invented by an English sailor, Peter Halket, in 1844. However, Assyrian special forces did use blown-up animal skins to cross rivers in the 8th century B.C. *Shopping carts* only arrived on the planet in the 20th century for use in supermarkets. *Traffic lights* were first introduced in the 19th century in Britain to allow Members of Parliament to cross the road safely. Viking houses had garbage heaps, but the first metal *garbage cans* turned up in Paris in the 19th century.

Pages 12–13

Electric fans first whirred in New York in 1882. Vikings had plenty of *ivory,* not from elephants, but from the tusks of walrus which they hunted. They also had plenty of chances to eat snow, but the first real frozen ices were made in Italy in the 16th century, while the first *ice cream* was made by a French chef for the English king Charles I. Europeans didn't learn how to make paper until the 12th century, so there were no *wastepaper baskets* in Byzantium.

Pages 14–15

Some Viking houses had sweating rooms that worked like a *sauna* – the more you sweated, the cleaner you got! *Pogo sticks* are a 20th-century invention. The Vikings had a full set of tools, including *saws*. Viking farmers found it easier to raise animals than grow crops, but they had *wooden plows* that could be pulled by an ox. They also kept herds of *reindeer* for their milk and meat.

Pages 16–17

Carvings of *skis* dating from 2500 B.C. have been found in Norway. Viking skis were made of wood and were used at the Battle of Oslo in A.D. 1200. Vikings used horns for cups, but not flat-bottomed *mugs*. Some Viking warriors drank out of their enemies' skulls to show how brave they were. The Vikings used *toboggans*, both dugouts and frames. The earliest *skates* (*above*) have been found among Viking remains and were made from carved bones – the Viking name for them means "ice leg bone."

Pages 18–19

The Romans invented the hypocaust, a sort of under-floor hot-air radiator, but the first modern *radiator* system was developed in 18th-century France. The Vikings just used fires to heat their

Catch the Thief

Now's the time to use your six clues to work out which of these Vikings (right) has stolen Odin's magic shield. Perhaps you saw one of them with the shield on pages 4–26? If you can't tell who the thief is from your clues, some of your answers must have been wrong. The answer is on page 32!

houses. The Vikings had ironing boards made out of whalebone, and *irons* made from lumps of heated glass. The Vikings didn't have *buttons,* but fastened their cloaks with brooches or pins passed through rings. Both Viking men and women wore *makeup.*

Pages 20–21

The Vikings did have *drums*, but at a funeral they beat out a rhythm on their shields. The ancient Egyptians wrapped their dead up as *mummies*, but Viking corpses were simply buried in their clothes. Until they became Christians, the pagan Vikings had no *priests* – at ceremonies the chieftain or father of the family doubled as a religious leader. The Vikings drank plenty of *beer* and drank their best brew – called Nabid – at funerals. *Movie cameras* were first used in the 1890s.

Pages 22–23

The Danish *flag* is one of the oldest in the world, dating back to the 1200s. However, Denmark was not yet a country during the Viking period. *Chainsaws* were invented in the 20th century. Drawings exist of a kind of *flamethrower* used by the Moors and Byzantines against Viking boats. These may have thrown Greek fire – a combustible

solution including sulfur and oil – which ignited when it hit the water. There were Saracen and Viking cavalry (*left*), but they wouldn't have worn *spurs* in a sea battle!

Pages 24–25

Viking children played on the turf roofs of Icelandic houses, but the *lawn mower* was only invented in England in 1830. Some say that *golf* was invented in Viking times, but the first definite records are from Scotland in the 16th century (*below*). *Polar bears* were hunted by Vikings in Greenland, but not Iceland and yes, the Vikings ate them! The Vikings believed in all kinds of magic, including male and female *witches* (who wouldn't have worn a tall black hat). *Bell ringers* were known throughout Europe from Roman times, but the Vikings used messengers to call people together.

Pages 26–27

A *leopard skin* is just the kind of exotic object the Vikings might have bought from traders from North Africa or Asia – but they wouldn't have gotten them in America. The North American peoples didn't ride *horses,* until they were brought by Europeans in the 16th century. *Turkeys* first came from America – maybe the Vikings saw some in

Vinland. *Paper money* was invented by the Chinese in about A.D. 800, but would not have been used by the Vikings.

True or False

Page 7 *False* – The longest longboat was 180 feet.

Page 11 *True* – Viking swords were given names like "Odin's Flame" or "Viper of the Enemy," arrows names like "The Glad Flyer," and helmets "War Boar!"

Page 13 *False* – Life was cheap in the medieval world. Young boys were often sold for just a goat or a fine cloak.

Page 16 *True* – *Berserkirs* roamed the country looking for fights. Many men, knowing they could not win, simply handed over their property to them.

Page 19 *True* – Runes had magical powers that could protect against magic!

Page 26 *True* – The first cows were brought to America by the Vikings and later by 16th century Spanish Conquistadors.

Play the Game
Once you have picked out the villainous thief, try your luck at the exciting Race Around the World game on pages 30–31.

Odo the Odious | Ulf Ax | Freda Forktongue | Sven Swinehead | Gunnhilda Snake | Bjorn Friggson | Olaf the Peacock | Frithiof the Foul | Wily Gudrun

Race Around the World

Rules of the Game

1 You must collect eight items (see trade chart on page 31) from ports around the world before Sven Swinehead does. All players and Sven start and finish at Hedeby.

2 Sven travels a set route, calling at Lake Ladoga, Novgorod, Constantinople, Ireland, Vinland, Greenland, Iceland, and North England. His counter moves three squares every turn, and as he has the sacred shield of Odin with him, he can ignore all dangers.

3 You have two choices of route. The first is the same as Sven's, but one with many dangers on the way. If you land on a red square, you must follow the instructions.

The second route is overland. This is slower, but you can pick up all eight items without crossing the Atlantic by calling at Bulgar, Baghdad, and Normandy.

4 You move first, throwing one die each turn, except on the purple overland route where you move one square each turn. If there is more than one player, the player with the longest name goes first.

5 For each item you lose, you must visit an extra port (e.g., Normandy) before returning to Hedeby.

6 The winner is the first to return to Hedeby with any eight trading items. But watch out – Sven is a fast mover!

Your Mission

The town of Hedeby cannot decide who is going to be the next chief. So the elders of the town set a challenge. You must travel to the far corners of the world and bring back eight items to prove your worth.

However, you must do this before evil Sven Swinehead or any other players get them first. Use plastic pieces, or make some from card with Viking designs.

Greenland

Iceland

Lost in Fog
Lose 2 turns while you work out which way to go.

L'Anse-aux-Meadows

Vinland

Winds Blow You South
Oh no, you have to sail past North America again!

Skraelings Attack!
Go back 3 squares while your arrow wounds heal. Ouch!

NORTH ATLANTIC

Boat Overturned by Whale
Disaster – 2 items are lost in the waves. Visit two extra ports before going home.

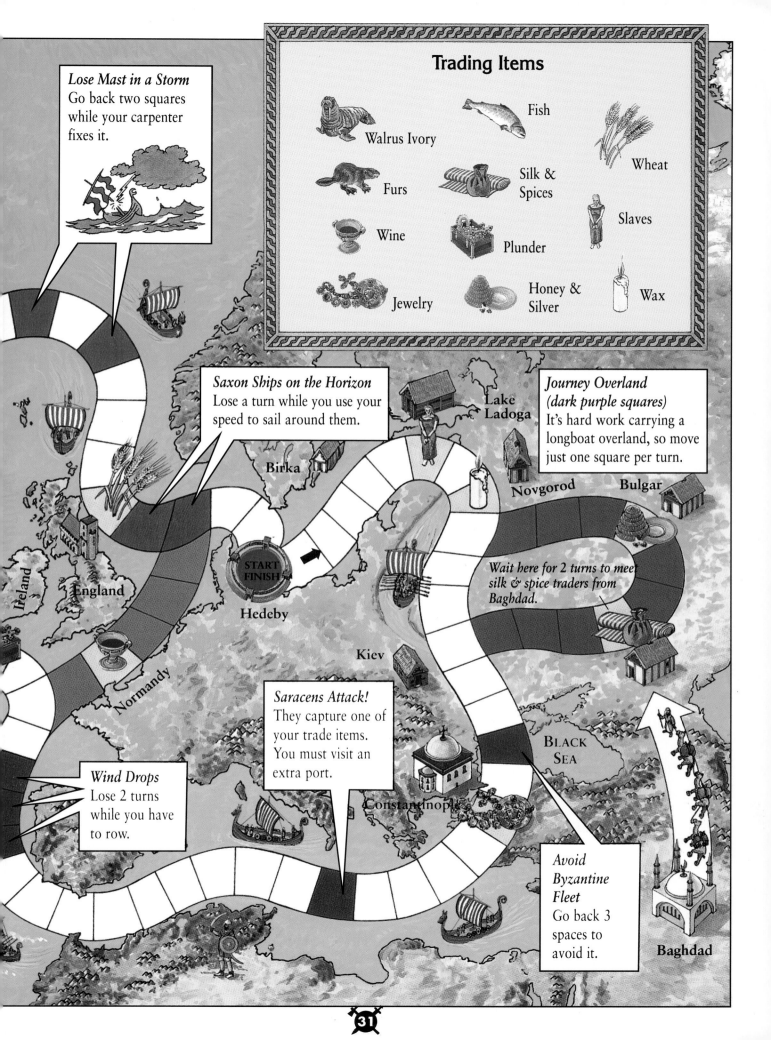

Trading Items

Walrus Ivory

Fish

Wheat

Furs

Silk & Spices

Wine

Plunder

Slaves

Jewelry

Honey & Silver

Wax

Lose Mast in a Storm
Go back two squares while your carpenter fixes it.

Saxon Ships on the Horizon
Lose a turn while you use your speed to sail around them.

Journey Overland (dark purple squares)
It's hard work carrying a longboat overland, so move just one square per turn.

Wait here for 2 turns to meet silk & spice traders from Baghdad.

Saracens Attack!
They capture one of your trade items. You must visit an extra port.

Wind Drops
Lose 2 turns while you have to row.

Avoid Byzantine Fleet
Go back 3 spaces to avoid it.

Lake Ladoga

Birka

Novgorod

Bulgar

START FINISH

Hedeby

Ireland

England

Kiev

Normandy

BLACK SEA

Constantinople

Baghdad

Index

No Escape for the Thief!

All along it was villainous Viking Sven Swinehead who had run off with the magic shield of Odin. Did you identify him? Turn to page 15 and you can even catch Sven hiding the shield in the woods (at the top of the page).

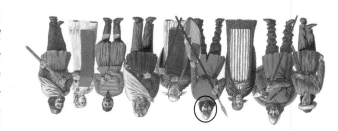